Maria Camelia

Special Women

2023
Cluj-Napoca

"To see Paradise in a wild flower"

William Blake

    I am Maria Camelia, a living spirit of spring and I discover myself through life experiences such as the child, the mother, the wild and wise woman, being present in everything I receive and give to others. Although I am named after the Camellia flower, I find myself more of a wild flower because wild flowers are unconfined and free.

    The stories of "special women" are inspired by my life experience, but also by my friends, whom I thank for the inspiration to write and for allowing me to be part of their lives. They are all special women to me, not because of their superiority, but because of their authenticity and uniqueness.

Thank you and I love you!

Once upon a time... is the beginning of all stories, only the stories in this book are true and they really were. They are real life experiences discovered in a moment of... pause... the pandemic moment, I will call it that because the whole world knows it. Then I stopped, got a front row ticket to the play of my life and sat comfortably in the audience seat. Now don't imagine that I was in a state of euphoria and delight, on the contrary, I was trapped in my own emotional web, disappointed with myself and tired of repeating the same relational pattern in which betrayal played the main role and injustice played the secondary one. I had been playing both of them very well for some time, for about 30 years now. Then I looked around, at the women in my family, at the women in my circle of friends, at the wives of my entourage, at my grandmothers and others... we were all in the same dance of fairies, holding hands with the need to be seen, appreciated, valued, supported, but co-dependent... some on spiderwebs, others on the ephemerality of sensational moments, others on pedestals or in hypnotic carousels, running again and again because it is stable, comfortable, familiar, but also illusory. Actresses on the big stage of life where the role of Special Woman suits us so well, emotionally wallowing in the euphoria of applause for an identity created in the darkness of the closet in order to have the spotlight on us.

All 7 stories, "The Fly in the Spider's Web", "The Sakura Warrior", "The Caterpillar and the Cocoon of Complexity", "The Illuminated Sunflower", "The Peacock in High Heels", "The Plasticine Goddess", "The Mouse and the Mirror Trap" " are actually a metamorphosis or a transformational journey. The stories are simple, but suggestive to create the picture in which there are the naive child, the lover hungry for recognition, the tireless mother, like the "elastic woman" and the great savior, all running in the great wheel of the mouse. Captive through the masks, the armor, the roles of "that's how it should be", or in the cages of status, etiquette, snobbery and false values, for fear of being left alone or worthless. I wrote these stories because I am certain that once they are read they will raise questions and even bring about change when it is truly desired. I wrote these stories because they can be valuable for women who keep going in the same circle. I wrote these stories because I feel and strongly believe that the simple break from endlessly repeating the same roles in the victim-abuser-rescuer triangle and running away from ourselves, is enough to pull back the curtain and decide if I want to choose the path of authenticity and inner truth.

Stories are alive, because they are lived and can be a means of introspection, but also of therapy for those who really want to choose the perspective of authenticity and inner truth. After all, we live by the stories that we tell ourselves...

The Fly in the spider web

I once passed by a group of kids who looked at me intently and I heard behind me how one of them said, "Look what a fly face this woman has". They all burst out laughing, so did I, but inside I couldn't wait to glance at myself in some mirror or car window. Thought and done. I was looking at my reflection in the car window and yes, they were right, with my big round white rimmed sunglasses I looked like a fly. This resemblance stuck in my mind. I thought it was funny. After a while I remembered her and I felt her as if someone had sent me a message, which I only now understand. The similarity is striking with what I experienced on my own skin. That's when I realized I was a fly in a spider's web. So, I was inspired to write this story.

Once upon a time, there was a fly that walked easily on the threads of a spider's web. Strange for a fly, flies usually get caught and remain stuck, awaiting their end as a prey. Well, this fly seemed to be at ease going up and down the sticky web threads. The spider, master of the web, seemed equally detached, as if it was natural for the fly to be there behaving like this. It seemed unusual to me and I became more attentive, stopped to notice what was actually happening. He, the spider, was like a king. The fly swarmed around him, served him, showed him through everything she did for him how wonderful she was and that she was not some prey. She thought she was very special and she wanted him to see that at all costs. She even learned new things, such as being able to walk on the threads of the web without getting stuck at all, which the other trapped flies couldn't do. She was appreciated by all the insects caught in the web. How great she was! In the evening, she was exhausted from all the work and attention she gave to the king, and in the morning she started all over again. She could reinvent herself for him, she could become whatever he wanted. One day she had the courage to tell him that she would like to stay with him forever, that she loves him beyond words and that they are meant to be together at any cost. Nothing else mattered to her but to be there, in his world, with him. She could sit looking at him for hours, she longed for his beautiful words, for his gentle touches, but... they were so rare and for such a short time, yet she lived them to the fullest, always hoping that he feels the same and that the long-awaited moment to be together will come. Time passed, and their moments together were rarer and shorter. The shorter they were, the more intensely she, the fly, lived them until exhaustion. Gradually she was losing weight, she was in pain, she saw other flies around the spider and lost hope, but he made sure that in those moments she stood by his side, making her feel that she was special, unique, only her. It was enough for her again, she was starting over, as if reviving her, she was getting another dose of attention, small, but how good it was. She was used to getting a little, after all, others flies didn't get any attention at all... and then there was him, the "king", and she was his secret "queen". His little attentions had become the center of the universe for the fly, she lived for those moments. Days went by, and he didn't see her, sometimes it was as if she didn't even exist... The greater his carelessness and indifference, the greater was her effort to capture his attention. She ended up in a sea of tears, sometimes she got angry and prepared revenge plans, sometimes she didn't answer him, pretended to be indifferent, but her soul was full of pain. One day, with tears in her

eyes, she looked to the sky, as if begging for divine help. An owl, from the branch of a nearby tree, began to speak to her.
- I have been looking at you for a while and I keep wondering how a fly with such beautiful wings lives on this sticky, disgusting web, next to a spider?
- I'm not a fly, I'm a female spider and I have no wings! The fly replied, somewhat disturbed by the owl's remarks.

The owl looked at her for a few moments, then continued:
- You can say whatever you think you are, but you are not yourself, your heart is full of pain, and then you may become nothing but pain. You've ended up feeding on pain, you're stuck in this damn web because you can't see your wings anymore. You forgot about yourself and who you really are because you wanted to be something you thought he was looking for. You cancelled yourself so much that you created a new identity for yourself, hoping that you will be the one, hoping that by being special you will make him see you, appreciate you. You even went so far as to manage to weave another web, you, a fly... And what did you get? Did you get anything in return? He doesn't even see it.
- Well, he doesn't see it, but I know that somewhere deep in his soul, he values me.
- He values you for what he needs, you want him to see you as his "queen", but he only wants a fly, he's a spider, and this is his web, the trap into which all flies fall.
- No fly has ever been like me, look, I even managed to turn into a spider, to weave a web, which is amazing, said the fly, proud of herself.
- We all like to see amazing things, they fascinate us, but not all of us know how to appreciate their value. We just want them as trophies that are rightfully ours, especially when we get them easily. I wonder what keeps you around him?
- I love him, he's my king, he's gentle and tender, childish, he talks to me nicely, he makes me feel special, we like the same things, he wants me... we're alike in many ways. I've never met anyone like him.
- Have you ever thought that he is doing all this to make you feel special and to keep you his prisoner? You called him your king because you put him on a pedestal and created a story about him, but really he's just a poor spider, that's what he does... he catches flies in his web. All flies are special to him, because they are trophies and it seems natural to him, it's his nature. But you... you want to

change the nature of things, because you are afraid to be you, a fly, nothing special, just something natural. As a fly, you could even be devoured or abandoned, alone... and... you begin to lose yourself in an illusory story. You thought that all your effort to be something you weren't, or something you thought he wanted, would bring you your happy ending... being the chosen one. Yes, you were chosen, but as a prey for later, when you get tired of fighting, showing, proving, validating yourself, compromising and sacrificing yourself in the name of an experience you call love.

- What else can it be if I was even able to transform myself for him?
- Addiction. Dependence on a spider that you have crowned as king, to rise to your level... and for you to validate yourself as queen. You have become addicted to your story, you yourself have become fascinated by your own creation. You love this canvas and everything you've created around so-called love, and you indulge in this game where the bigger the challenge, the more interesting it is for you. You created a false kingdom because being a fly you are alone. The idea of having a different ending than the one you expected seems unfair for all the effort you've put in. It would be unthinkable to be rejected, abandoned, unappreciated, unseen, unwanted... what would you be then?
- I don't know... said the fly sadly... and I don't even know what I should do to find out...
- Remember yourself... you are a fly, with wings, wings that can unfold and take flight from the spider's web... Fly on the first leaf that comes your way and take your time, look at yourself from another perspective and seek to discover yourself by loving yourself first.

Your story page

What is your "Spider web"? What is the situation/event/people/ that you feel are blocking you?
Describe what the "fly" does to feel special? The more detail you describe, the clearer your situation will be.
Very important! Be honest!
Observe and accept every behavior!
Don't judge or blame yourself, or you will end up victimizing yourself like the fly in its dialogue with the owl.
What will help you is detachment, looking at yourself and your story from the outside.
You are wonderful as you are, even being "a fly".

The Sakura Warrior

Sakura or the Japanese cherry blossom says that... life is fleeting. The beauty of this flower that lasts for a very short time makes me think of it as being special. A butterfly, a sunset, a sky with foamy clouds, a cherry blossom, a poppy, a lightning, a season... I could continue with examples of maximum intensity of moments that are ephemeral... Then there is the desire to keep them and to live them to the fullest because they seem special to us and the more special we see them, the more we want them. It's a vicious circle and a paradox. They are like a drug, they become an addiction, and some of us search for them all our lives, and even identify with them. It's very painful when you realize that you are clinging to something so ephemeral, but at the same time it seems unique to you, and that feeds the need to be special. If you stopped for a moment from the search for the sensational, for the experiences that take your breath away, you could see the beauty of life in its very banality, integrating all the moments you live, not just the ones that seem unique to you.

The cherry blossom flower in the story to be played, fell in love in a spring. It was blooming time, when looking at the cherry blossoms took your breath away. He, a fighter, tough, fearless, seemed to move mountains, her samurai, that's what she called him. It was a bumblebee. She saw him among the flowering branches, he admired her, their eyes met and she could not forget him. It was the moment she wished she could live on, not die like her other flower sisters, and offer him her cup full of nectar for eternity. She told herself then that she had to find a way to show her samurai that their meeting was no coincidence and that she deserved to be loved. This gradually became a goal in her life. She even began to transform herself into a samurai, she trained almost daily, she had become a skilled fighter, she could face even other samurai who did not believe in her skill. At the same time she wanted to remain a flower, so that he could see her tenderness, her uniqueness. But, he was implacable, he had standards that he could not give up and other flowers whose cup could not be refused, he had backbone, but not vertically. The more untouchable he was, the more she struggled to find ways and situations to be and look more special. All her gifts were now on a platter which she offered along with her heart full of love. Her heart had become like the petals of a cherry blossom, sensitive to touch, radiant with freshness and vitality when she was around him. She looked around at the other cherry blossoms and pitied them, she didn't understand why they allowed themselves to wither and fall. They were so beautiful... no, no, no... She wasn't going to last that short, she was going to last forever, she had to find a way to stay special in order for him to see her. Sometimes, she amplified his small gestures, taking them as evidence of love, in fact they were crumbs of attention for which she offered maximum energy, enough to charge her until the next time. Of course, the discharge moment followed, like the battery... and it was... extremely... painful. Time passed, the cherry blossom, fearless, saw her reflection in the crystal clear water of a pond after a warm rain. Her petals fell smoothly to the ground, leaving her empty. She was just a sweet, fleeting flower, and he was a bumblebee in search of nectar, pollinating cherry blossoms, of course. Nothing special, nothing out of the ordinary. Her expectations were falling like soft petals. What the beautiful cherry blossom didn't see, yet, was the small fruit that was emerging from all the love she was capable of and beyond the dependence on her uniqueness was the living that made her alive... And that all the bumblebees, the samurai or all the fearless fighters in this world cannot establish your uniqueness or identity, but only your natural state of being, even if it is ephemeral, like a cherry blossom.

Your story page

Look in your life for the situations/people/experiences that are ephemeral, but you are clinging to them at all costs?
Describe the situations, everything you remember, in all aspects. Then read them again and let yourself feel. How do you see the situation now? Describe all the images, feelings, people, as if you were in the theater and witnessing a play.
When did you feel like you were turning into a warrior for a fight that is actually your own need to be special? For a "bumblebee"...?
Remember that moment in your life when you were a "cherry blossom" in full bloom and you felt wonderful, just because you were you, an ephemeral cherry blossom, but with a wonderful fruit lying inside you... and live it again.

The caterpillar and the cocoon of complexity

To know! Searching continuously, fervently for the meaning of life keeps you in a restlessness that creates a commotion, a struggle, and the more you want to know, to find answers that satisfy you, the more restless you are, you can't stop searching, you seem to be hungrier for knowledge. And you weave, you weave, you weave endlessly like a caterpillar weaving its own cocoon, and even when the metamorphosis takes place and it becomes a butterfly, it realizes that it has actually entered another cocoon, and then another, in a vastness of the cocoon of the Universe itself... In short, a tangle! Elegantly said, a complexity, but no, not in the scientific sense, but emotionally... you are creating a complication, from which you end up not understanding anything at all. What actually defines you? The complexity! But things are so simple... the process is natural: larva, caterpillar, cocoon, butterfly, full stop... and... Then back from the beginning. But, no, it can't be that simple, something must occur... a mystery, something special.

These were the thoughts of a special caterpillar, always studying. Every rib in the leaf, shape, color, taste, spore, every detail was studied, researched, questioned, compared, "split into 16" under the microscope of the tireless mind. Theories, experiments, scientific research, pragmatic approaches, mysticism, shamanism and other –isms… all passed through her synapses. It was so beautiful when a crumb of truth was revealed… Evrika! Shouted the caterpillar and started all over again, hungrier and hungrier for knowledge. She was still alone all the time, but she didn't feel it because the search had become her partner. She also had days when she received attention, was courted, but what a pity, the tempters did not rise to the level of her "hunger" for knowledge. " How can you be so superficial? Just reproduction, nothing more? But the meaning of life? To know who you are, why you came into this world?" Existential questions that did not quite reach the reception area of the males around her, did not find the frequency. Paradoxically, the more they were, the more she isolated herself, she found fault with everyone and weaved, weaved, weaved in her own cocoon. Even the ones who seemed to know how to read the stars to discover the mystery, were not complex enough. Why should she come down after being able to climb so high! Excluded! All they had to do is take on the responsibility!

Well, that's how the internal dialogue of the caterpillar unfolded, who after all this fluttering, stopped in its tracks longing for a… simple hug. Then she no longer wanted to know, only to feel. It was the time of the simple whys, but not like those of curious children, but from feelings of unfulfillment, unhappiness, lack of love, no, no, no. Questions she wasn't getting answered, as she expected. The caterpillar wove its cocoon with silk thread from the complexity of thoughts and feelings, until the cocoon had become special, complex. Ah! She couldn't wait to turn into a butterfly, she was sure to be a complex, special butterfly. Then she will surely be seen, appreciated at her true value, and surely the mystery will be discovered. A mind as complex and brilliant as hers is sure able to think of something new. The cocoon was ready. Prepared by the sleep of transformation, the caterpillar took a break, a break from all the searching, the tumult, and the anxieties. The thrill of knowledge stopped for a while in a complex cocoon. What followed was a deep stillness, a natural stillness for an end to complexity and a birth of the simplicity of a moth butterfly… simple, natural, perfectly integrated into the rhythms of Mother Earth.

…and when you think that for the ancient Greeks the word butterfly means "soul"… For you, wonderful caterpillar, "soul"… what does it mean?

Your story page

What is the "cocoon of complexity" in your life?
It's very cool to have a complex cocoon and always seek answers to existential questions as long as you don't isolate yourself from the world hoping that makes you special and therefore seen.
If you have found situations similar to the cocoon in your life, describe them, write, write, write and release them.
Then stop and let yourself feel how you are, reconciled and at peace, or not. Why are you at peace and for which reasons are you not?
What keeps you in the cocoon and doesn't let you turn into a butterfly? Where did you get stuck?
What would have to happen for you to become a "butterfly"?
Remember that you were once a butterfly, a wonderful one, feel that moment and relive it.

The illuminated Sunflower

The sun! The king of light and heat! How can you not love him? How can you not turn around for him? Ever worshiped, the Sun is the definition of brilliance and light. "You are the sun of my life!" or "My sun!" or "You are my Sun Ray!" all dedicated to the incomparable, immeasurable, omniscient and omnipotent Sun. It would have been unthinkable for him not to have a flower of his own, which amazingly, perfectly resembles him. An earthly match for the celestial sun star. The divine plan is perfect! A unique seed that gives birth through the nourishment of sunlight to a multitude of seeds filled with nourishing oil. You see her in the field with her faces, turning their golden corollas seeking Him, the one, bright sun, all alike, all to worship and bestow.

However... among them all, there is one, one in a million, that is not like all the others... it is special! Ever since she was little she loved to be bathed in his rays, she adored him and was always sad when he hid behind the clouds. A burning desire grew in her to rise to his level of brilliance and power, to see her, to become illuminated, so she could be his mate. That alone could secure the star's attention. She looked for him every day, he was always in her thoughts, she wouldn't have imagined it any other way. He was the only one who could give her fulfillment and he had to be hers, only hers, but for that she had to prepare herself, illuminate herself and shine for him to see. There followed moments, hours, days, weeks, months, years in which she "refined herself", read, learned, attended courses, and even had various love experiences, different races, cultures, all to become a teacher, an initiate. She was tireless, greedy for knowledge, unstoppable in exploration, she had become fearless, but obsessed with being an Ascended. He always showed her how great, erudite, knowledgeable she was. Sometimes she daydreamed about how he would look at her and flood her with his light, how he would fill her with his beneficial solar energy and she offered herself to him unconditionally. An orgasm in all its illusory splendor, but good. That's how the sunflower's days unfolded, in a beautiful psychosis. All this time, beyond the veil of illusion, the solar king, habitually went about his life, rising, shining, illuminating, nourishing, warming, and setting at the end of the day, natural, unique for all the flowers, with all the names, of all possible species and varieties.

But... because all stories have lessons to teach, the sunflower also had her moment of grace. One day, precisely on her birthday, the Sun was not in the sky. A gloomy, dark day, with thick dark, watery clouds covering the sunlight. She waited in vain all day for a sign from him, at least a ray, a glimmer no matter how small... just as the cricket begged from the ant... "a seed how small", but nothing. The golden petalled corolla of the sunflower bowed heavily to the ground, disappointed, tired, not understanding how it was possible for him not to remember her, to forget this day so important to her... At one point, a bee sat down on one of the petals making her pay attention to what was happening around her. All her other sister-creatures were in exactly the same state, they were all experiencing the same sadness, rainy, gloomy, disappointed... in SHOCK! She was not unique, special, not even

illuminated as she had thought... They were all the same, Flowers of the Sun. All sought his light in order to be happy, radiant, fulfilled, but the source of their well-being was outside themselves. Without him, it was like there was nothing left. Well, after every moment of real "enlightenment" comes the state of denial. It's impossible, there's no way, it cannot be true, impossible for him not to have seen me, noticed me... Isn't it obvious that I vibrate higher than the others? But the gloomy and cloudy days continued and the sad sunflower began to rebel, she even hated her solar king, she promised herself that she would never come back for him, she gave herself to him, every moment of her life it was for him, and what about her? What did she get? She deserved everything, just for her. There were long times of turmoil and unanswered questions for the beautiful sunflower, until the day when a tiny grain of seed broke from its shell giving the solar energy to the earth and its living things. The one moment he kept reading about in all the writings but never experienced... giving and receiving are one and the same. The sun with its light was in all her seeds, waiting for the moment of ripening for giving, being hers and all the flowers. And... Take note, beautiful flower, the enlightenment is within you, don't look for it outside of yourself because you might realize how mundane and natural it is.

Your story page

Enlightenment, rising, ascension, omniscience, omnipotence, omnipresence, master and everything that leads you to think of something higher, of power, of knowledge, beyond the material plane, just to be special, just because that's how you are seen, appreciated, loved, forcing yourself to be something you are not... all these grand ideals are your ego trying its best to gain an identity, as long as they are outwardly oriented.
The Sunflower and the Sun characters are purposely chosen to bring out our need to be special in us. It seems that the level of arrogance increases in direct proportion to the level of false "enlightenment".
Who are you without the "sun" in your life? The sun can be anything or anyone that makes you stick to standards, just to be recognized and special.
What are you without his attention?
Look for moments of arrogance or superiority in your life and observe your behavior. What are you actually missing?
How do you manifest when the "sun" enters the clouds?
Have you ever had a moment in your life when you just sat there listening to others and just being there for them? What did you feel?
Describe all your experiences, how others behaved, what memory did you have after the moment?
Write the story of your own "enlightenment".
You are wonderful as you are "illuminated", but you don't need any "sun" to see that

The Peacock in high heels

The Peacock feathers... what a splendor! The legend says that when God created the birds, due to the pride of the peacock, he said: "Let your name be peacock and mean pride, and instead of creating a song, may you only scream." From then on the peacock remained with its proud feathers, but without a beautiful voice, only screaming. Yes, but the elegance, the beauty of the plumage, the incomparable way in which it unfolds its tail with feathers like a fan, are its indisputable qualities. It really fascinates you, you are as if hypnotized by its uniqueness. You would spend hours glued to the bars of the cage watching him..

...then suddenly a white peacock appears, of rare elegance, slow moving, gentle and proud. She walks infrequently, staring into the pool water, rolling her eyes, lengthening her thighs and undulating her hips. The slender legs look even longer because of the high-heeled shiny shoes. Apparently she feels very good about herself, she is looked at, admired, the peacocks swarm around her, some bolder ones dare to approach her, but her evaluative glances make them small, falling at her endless feet, kissing the soles of her varnished shoes. Others spread their tails dizzyingly, in a wonderful mixture of turquoise and emerald green, maybe this time they will manage to win the heart of the majestic peacock female. It is true, she is of rare beauty, of royal blood, she would deserve someone of her rank, and never mind that her admirers are capable, imposing, some even very wealthy... but... She is special! One peacock in a million! She doesn't give in so easily to anyone, they have to meet some criteria, she has her standards. No matter how hard the peacocks tried to impress her, they couldn't reach above the peak of her high-heeled, shiny shoes. Well, they were too short, softies, without rich feathers, not corpulent enough. Countless suitors wandered past her cage, but none was the one of her dreams. During the day she seemed to have the world at her feet, but at night, she cried and lied alone in her satin bed, waiting for her hero who would deserve her uniqueness and special way of being. She had a few adventures, but after a short time she abandoned them out of boredom... they were not the one from her dreams. Time passed, she saw her friends who had a family, children, well-being, joy in their lives... and that's exactly what she wanted, but still not like that, not with anyone.

Perched on the high heels of her shoes she seemed untouchable. She saw some peacocks around that she would have liked, but either they already had females, or they were not interested in her, they did not see her, or she, let's face it, did not lower the standards. She didn't understand. She was beautiful, tall, slender, elegant, gentle, bright like the sun... How could they not see her? How could you not stop admiring a being like her, how could you not want to know her? Nonsense! They don't even know what they're missing! This is how she wondered every night, then, after a while, she began to wonder if fate, bad luck, was to blame... In fact, she began to look for answers in various more advanced sources. All the answers were the same! You are an extraordinary, unique being, you have nothing to worry about! That was unbelievable!

And yet she was alone... unfulfilled, a sad queen in her crystal palace with her beautiful male model floating on a cloud in her dreams.
One morning, as she was getting ready to put on her famous high-heeled slippers, they were nowhere to be found. She searched desperately for them for a while, asking if anyone had seen them, but to no result. Tired and exhausted, she went out barefoot, feeling the earth beneath her bare feet. It was for the first time that she felt alive, something in her body trembled and for the first time in a long time she spread her tail of pearly white feathers in a dizzying fan, just for her, just for her joy. She no longer wanted to be special, she wanted to be her, a white peacock, unique in her individuality.

Your story page

At what point in your life did you put on "Shiny shoes"?
Describe how you looked physically, how you thought, what you felt in your heart?
How did you behave with the people around you?
What were the most important aspects of your life? What did it matter then?
Write the story of the peacock in you, be specific, be honest and don't let a single comma slip! Then...
....remember the beauty within you, let it flow through all your cells, take off your shiny shoes and walk barefoot. Let the earth kiss your feet and feel...

The plasticine goddess

I really love the Goddesses, you notice them easily, because in their case everything must be big, imperial, sumptuous, above the clouds, above everything... right?! Big house, big car, "big" man, big family, everything "big". The goddess in this story is a real Artemis, who ends up erecting her own statue, only clay plasticine is not the happiest material to support her. Here's how the entire artwork unfolded...

Cat-like, the Goddess cuddled flatteringly using honeyed words, watching his reactions out of the corner of her eye. He, her superior, an enlightened and highly spiritual God, a true ascended master, was impenetrable. The iron mask on his face fascinated her, even more than that, the armor around his heart, titanium no other, challenged her. But how perfect it was for her! She wanted him because he lived up to her standards, lived up to her drive, the more impenetrable he was, the more he challenged her. Beauty and the Beast or The Taming of the Shrew, only the shrew was a he. The story was created quickly. She always wanted someone who would make her feel alive to the core. She enticed him with her body, with her soft, white, pearly skin, perfect shapes and the natural sensuality of a Goddess. Oh! How good it was!... for a while. He was hers, only for her, as she had always dreamed of him.

 A God and a Goddess making love, what could be more wonderful? They even moved in together... he moved to her place. They were one big happy family! She, the Goddess, was at the peak of happiness, she made sure that everything was to everyone's liking, she cooked, she took care of the house, the children, the expenses, the vacation plans, so that everyone was happy and comfortable. She was sometimes a mother, sometimes a lover, sometimes a housewife, sometimes a businesswoman, sometimes a great fighter for justice, she was everything to everyone... He, the God, was served, because the Goddess made sure that everything was perfect, after all he was a God. However, the moments of love were rarer and rarer, the conversations more and more trivial, and the silences between them more and more frequent... But she was strong, she hadn't done enough, she didn't let herself be knocked down, she had to try even harder, to think of other ways to get the situation back on track. She soon realized that the only thing that worked was the weapon of seduction, it still worked, then it was good. But it was cruel! All her struggle, all the effort, sacrifice, inventiveness, everything she had done to not give up on her story, on her love... all the foundation on which she had built her love was made of plasticine, of modelling clay. She allowed herself to be shaped by others in the hope that they would see her, appreciate her, for her true worth. She was able to build her own statue, but plasticine is not the best material for it. The Goddess Artemis, was oozing at her feet, exhausted, tired of loving and sacrificing and being a Goddess for a man she put on a pedestal and making a God out of him only to validate herself as a Goddess. Except, a hardened God can't love a plasticine Goddess... the materials aren't compatible.

The "love" story was falling apart before her eyes and she didn't understand why. Why does that happen when you love and you want everything to be good for everyone, why are your expectations not met? What's more, you feel unloved and you feel small, unappreciated, unvalued, everything falls apart and you don't know what to do, you become helpless, as if everything is in vain... and where can you find that gram of lucidity in which to see the harsh truth? The goddess Artemis with truth and justice in her sheath is struck down by her own weapons.

The truth is that... your own good is not always the good of others, compromised love is not love, big does not mean good, power does not mean maximum effort, a man is not only a God, a woman is not only a Goddess, a relationship of love is a continuous alternation between the prince and the beggar, and at least two persons must be involved in a love story.

Love does not mean proving how lovable you are, but being lovable, to love, and if you don't feel loved, to free yourself. Then start loving yourself first.

Your story page

Look for the situation in your life when you felt like the plasticine Goddess of a God. When you "shaped" yourself to his liking, just because you wanted to be seen, appreciated, loved, sometimes maybe just to be... because, only through what you did for him, you existed and had an identity.
Describe every detail of the saviour Goddess in you, who reconciles everyone, wants everyone to be well, just to make herself feel good or to confirm her own worth.
Remember a time in your life when, being alone, you felt like you were a wonderful goddess without waiting for anyone's approval. When you have truly seen yourself, without the expectations or confirmations of others, even if they are Gods!
The "pedestal" in your heart has no value, except the one you will give to it! There, perhaps, among the ruins you will truly see yourself and begin to build!

The mouse and the mirror trap

Sometimes when we look in the mirror we prefer to see a different image of ourselves than the real one, we like to lie to ourselves and want to keep the same image by just changing the mirror. And we are sure that if our image is distorted, the mirror is to blame. Then another fantastic thing happens, we become so obsessed with the image in the mirror that we would do anything to keep it the way we want it, regardless of the consequences, caught in our own trap. This is what happens with the characters in the following story...

It was a sunny day, a lovely time to get out of the house! The little mouse, however, was very gloomy. There was also that meeting that she had promised to attend to, without fail. It was a quite interesting meeting between little mice, with teachings of art, dear to her soul. With all the sadness and bad mood, she heads for the meeting place. What happened there changed her life. Among countless mice, she saw a charming one, handsome, tall, imposing, the kind of male that takes your breath away and with whom you would go to the end of the world with, her type. They looked deep into each other's eyes, into the depths of their souls, saw their wounds with their pains and reached the most sensitive and unattainable limits of their feelings. It was magical. Then the game began. She called it love. Her soul vibrated at the mere image of him in her mind, he didn't have to be present. She was living something she had never lived before. Something connected them, she began to discover herself differently, and she liked it. He only had to be present, she did everything. He visited her from afar, made her feel wanted, special. They found a nest far away from the eyes of the world, in a world only theirs, as if from love stories. The moments were intense, but only lasted for as long as he could stay. Then days of sadness and longing followed. The little mouse was left alone feeding on memories. She also had beautiful moments when she felt inspired, she was very creative and she liked this state like a dose of adrenaline. But she also had moments of clarity, when the image of the male with the heart of a lion, with whom she fell in love, took the shape of a greedy man. Even so, she continued to love him, to give herself to him, to do everything in such a way as to be with him. Nothing mattered anymore except for him. Her family and friends were somewhere in the background, she went over her head to arrange everything to be with him, whenever the opportunity arose. She was a true master of improvisation. The beautiful nest at first, was gradually turning into a mouse trap... and she could see it because she was fully participating in its creation. She had even reached the performance of being able to survive there with only the crumbs of moments she received from him. She was there for him, at his disposal, she would let herself be caught, he would put his paw on her, then let her go, apparently, then come back for another game. She was making plans, showing him how many things they could do if they went together outside the nest. It was a turning point, the moment when the greedy mutt started to make some calculations... realizing that it's

not just a game anymore and that it's not worth it. His visits became rarer, the nice words turned into sharp words, and all this time the Little Mouse was waiting politely, lovingly, sadly in her trap. She didn't understand. She asked questions, wrote letters, but the story was no longer shaping up according to her expectations. Of course he had another Mouse in another trap, after all he was a tomcat. After a long time, in which sadness and disappointment left its mark on her beautiful face, she began to understand and see that she actually loved her own abuser... a tomcat. Gradually the pain began to work its way through the cracks of the rejection wounds. Still she couldn't give him up. Once she even got really sick to get attention, going so far as to think she couldn't live without him. Life had no meaning anymore, just because she couldn't bear the pain of rejection. She would have accepted all his cowardice out of the same cowardice... as she didn't have the courage to give up on something that was never hers. Getting out of her own trap was painful and long-lasting because she had to face reality, but there was a lesson she definitely learned:

Love is more than a game of seduction and that the lion-hearted male in the mirror may just be a greedy tomcat.

Your story page

When was the last time you looked into the mirror of your heart? What did you see?

What is your mouse trap? Look carefully for what keeps you spinning in the same wheel?

Describe in detail the situation in your life that keeps repeating itself and you reach the same result.

What compromises did you make to keep the lion in the mirror even though there was a greedy mutt next to you?

What benefits does stagnation bring you in the trap? Look for what you lack and delude yourself into thinking you are getting it.

Remember a time in your life when you felt wonderful just for being you, natural, without a mirror to reflect you. Describe the moment and feel it in your heart. That was you, a brave, real, wonderful, woman!

Healing... epilogue

The 7-headed dragon at the root is the same, at the top multiplied, 7 facets of the same state, only that, in different situations, with different people, it manifests itself differently. The dragon is special under 7 different manifestations and its heads can multiply, even regenerate if not cut off. As in Ispirescu's fairy tale, you need a good sword edge and a brave person to fight the dragon. All the 7 stories I wrote are actually one and the same, and the hero in the story is none other than the courage to recognize, be aware and "cut off" the pattern that brings you to run the same program which is BEING SPECIAL for someone in particular, with the goal of getting attention, recognition, validation, proving and showing that you deserve all his love. Just like at the market! You place the goods beautifully, washed, fresh and appetizing, to catch the buyer's eye. The energy invested in being more special than you already are by your uniqueness is called marketing and it is temporary, superficial, fleeting and ephemeral, and more often than not it brings with it a lack of identity or worse, a false identity. Do you change from who you are to who you are not, then you no longer recognize yourself and wonder who you really are? A wheel in which you keep spinning endlessly, until you decide to stop, to take a break... the blessed break, the holy moment, when everything seems to stop and you begin to see, awakened from a deep sleep, but not by a prince like in The Sleeping Beauty, but by the dragon in you. It starts popping its heads up, one after the other, through the life experiences you have. Now, it's the moment when you have a choice, you're Prince Charming with the sword in his hand or you go around nicely and put it on Repeat, re-entering the wheel and the same story.

Maria Camelia - *Special Women*

I have always admired the courage of the poppy flower, sensitive and gentle, yet so wild and powerful in its appearance. She is so special and so herself! She has a naturalness that fascinates and inspires, she is magnetic and has style, simple and present. Do you get it? That is what makes her stand out, her naturalness, her perfect integration into the wilderness where she grows. It has its moment of grace, when it fills you with the joy of the color of the red fields, then it leaves... giving way to the fruits of useful seeds, another stage of the same process. Yes, she is special, but she does nothing to be seen, appreciated, noticed, valued, she just is, either photographed, or written in verse, painted in paintings, sewn on clothing, immortalized everywhere. Her spirit is alive! It's something beyond shape and color, it's a state, an experience that fills you. Shortly after I wrote the stories I knew that all the characters, in their need to be special, cry out for love. All these characters were heads of the dragon in me that guarded the red poppy flower in my heart. My fears that I'm not enough, that I don't know or know enough, that I'm special and deserve more, that I can reinvent myself only for the sake of him, that I forget myself and sacrifice myself unnecessarily for the sake of everyone, until exhaustion. I was both victim and executioner, even savior, I carried burdens that are not mine, some I still carry, but I stopped for a moment, I put STOP. And I returned to the red thread of life and looked at myself, at everything that I am not, keeping only the poppy and everything that makes me feel alive, authentic, only for myself, giving myself, in order to have something to give to others. Then I did something else, I took off the "courage coat" and faced my dragon, head after head, I'm still doing it, it's MAGNIFICENT! With the first it is more difficult, but I invoke the fiercest, to set an example for the others. It's like a domino, it leaves you with a feeling of liberation. Then I thank them, because they are all really gifts in disguise. I don't regret anything and I believe that life is about spiraling up and down, not to sink, but to gain momentum and heal in order to remember your true self!

... so, this is it folks...
These are the stories of women who, no matter how special they are, are pearls that are polished through life experiences. Stories are alive, we create them, we live them, but we can also rewrite them and live them differently. The story is something with which life begins, beyond words, it is the place where dreams, desires or creations are born... it is both present and past but also future. It grows with me, comfort me, heals me, rejoices me and re-creates me. I can tell it as many times as I want, the same one over and over, or I can stop and change it, it's my choice. May these stories inspire you and give you time, just for a moment, for a well-deserved pause....

www.ingramcontent.com/pod-product-compliance
Lightning Source LLC
Chambersburg PA
CBHW042029100526
44587CB00029B/4351